DAD,
more than
a *little*

I more than a little *appreciate* you,
and the person you are,
and the things that you do.

It's true that you're generous
and funny and nice,
but you're *much* more than that...
you have shaped my whole life.

And the things that you've shown me by being yourself
have *taught* me much more than anything else.

Like how *big-heartedness* is its own kind of strength—
and that time spent together is everything.

I look back at our *brilliant* collection of days
and see so many things that I want to replay...

The *adventures* we had, and the *fun* that we shared,
your humor, your wisdom, your kindness, your care.

What made the *small* things feel so special and huge?
It's the fact that I got to do each one with you.

And you might be surprised
that through all of the years,
it's the *everyday* moments
I hold the most dear.

I once thought there was nothing that you couldn't do.
You know what? I *still* sometimes think that that's true.

And now that I'm older, I look back and see all the *work* you put in just to benefit me.

There's so much that I know
I would never have *tried*
if you hadn't been there at the time,
by my side.

More than I think you might ever quite know,
your *support* is still with me wherever I go.

Dad, so much of the person I've grown up to be
is because of the ways that you *guided* me.

I'm more than a little bit *grateful*, it's true...

for the good in my life

that exists thanks to you.

I'm writing these words to you,

straight from my heart:

Dad, thank you for everything

that you are.

COMPENDIUM®

live inspired

Written by: M.H. Clark

Illustrated by: Cécile Metzger

Edited by: Amelia Riedler

Art Direction by: Chelsea Bianchini

ISBN: 978-1-957891-08-8

1st printing. Printed in China with soy inks on FSC®-Mix certified paper.

Create meaningful moments with gifts that inspire.

CONNECT WITH US

live-inspired.com | sayhello@compendiuminc.com

@compendiumliveinspired
#compendiumliveinspired